PICTURE LIBRARY

PLANETS

PICTURE LIBRARY

PLANETS

SMS LMC

1003035

N. S. Barrett

Franklin Watts

London   New York   Sydney   Toronto

© 1985 Franklin Watts Ltd

First published in Great Britain
    1985 by
Franklin Watts Ltd
12a Golden Square
London W1

First published in the USA by
Franklin Watts Inc
387 Park Avenue South
New York
N.Y. 10016

First Published in Australia by
Franklin Watts
1 Campbell Street
Artarmon, NSW 2064

UK ISBN: 0 86313 283 9
US ISBN: 0-531-10005-7
Library of Congress Catalog Card
Number: 85-50159

Printed in Italy

Designed by
Barrett & Willard

Photographs by
NASA
Hale Observatories
McDonald Observatories, Texas
Novosti Press Agency

Illustrated by
Janos Marffy
Stuart Willard

Technical Consultants
Heather Couper
Nigel Henbest

Contents

Introduction

The Earth is a planet. It is one of nine planets that go around the Sun. Planets travel around the Sun in paths called orbits. They are held in their orbits by the great force exerted by the Sun. This is called gravitational force.

The planets vary in size. Four are smaller than the Earth, while the other four are very much larger.

△ The beautiful giant planet Saturn is encircled by a number of rings. One of Saturn's many moons, Rhea, can be seen as a tiny dot below the planet.

The planets are satellites of the Sun. Some planets themselves have satellites, or moons. The Earth has one. The planet Saturn has as many as 20 moons.

The Sun, the planets and their moons together make up the Solar System. Unmanned spacecraft called probes have been sent into space to explore the Solar System.

△ A picture of the surface of Mars sent back by a space probe that landed on the planet. The color of its rocky soil gives Mars its reddish appearance when seen in the night sky.

The Solar System

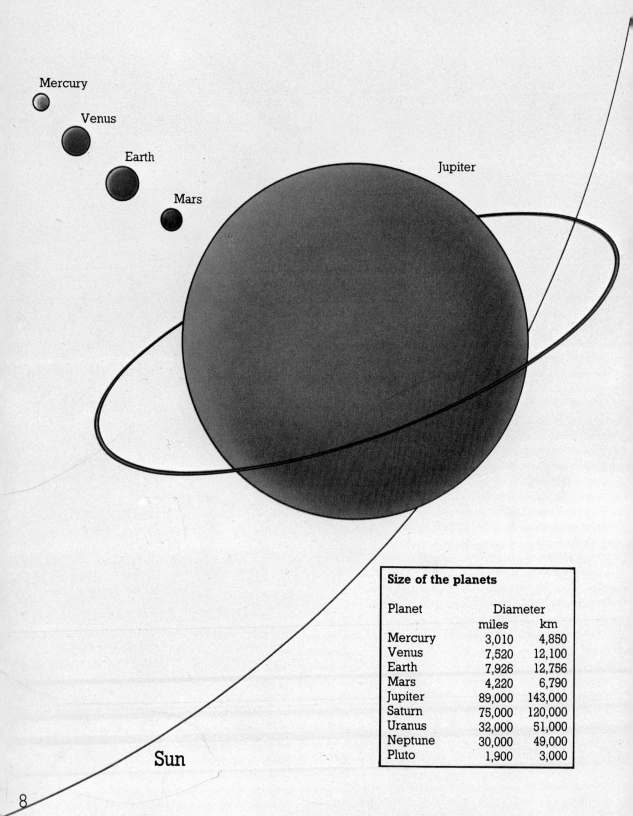

Mercury

Venus

Earth

Mars

Jupiter

Sun

Size of the planets		
Planet	Diameter	
	miles	km
Mercury	3,010	4,850
Venus	7,520	12,100
Earth	7,926	12,756
Mars	4,220	6,790
Jupiter	89,000	143,000
Saturn	75,000	120,000
Uranus	32,000	51,000
Neptune	30,000	49,000
Pluto	1,900	3,000

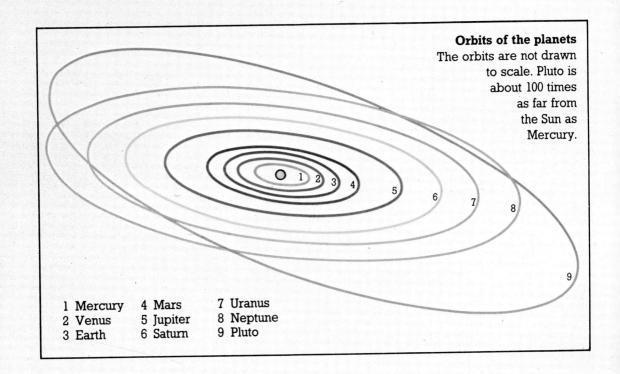

Orbits of the planets
The orbits are not drawn to scale. Pluto is about 100 times as far from the Sun as Mercury.

1 Mercury	4 Mars	7 Uranus
2 Venus	5 Jupiter	8 Neptune
3 Earth	6 Saturn	9 Pluto

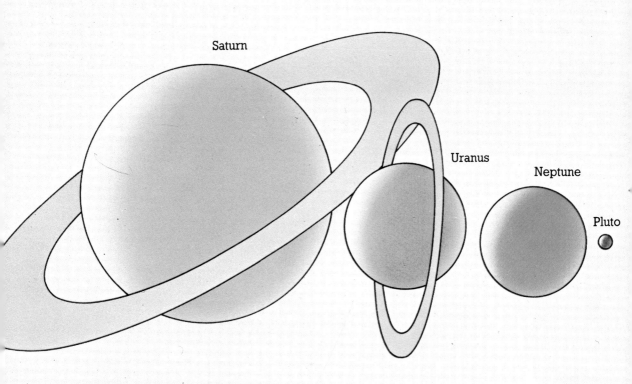

Saturn

Uranus

Neptune

Pluto

The Earth

The Earth is the third planet from the Sun. Only Mercury and Venus move in orbits closer to the Sun.

Like the other planets, the Earth spins around on its axis, an imaginary line that goes through it from top to bottom. The time it takes to spin around once is called a day. The time it takes to go around the Sun is called a year.

△ The Earth as seen from space. The continent of Africa occupies the upper left part of the globe and dense white cloud covers most of the South Pole.

Of all the planets and moons in the Solar System, only the Earth is able to support forms of life as far as we know. The other bodies are either too hot or too cold, too large or too small to provide the special conditions necessary for life.

Water is important to life. So is the atmosphere, the blanket of air that surrounds the Earth. It provides oxygen for breathing, and it holds the Sun's heat in at night.

▽ The Moon is Earth's companion in space. This picture was taken from the Moon. The shining crescent in the night sky is Earth.

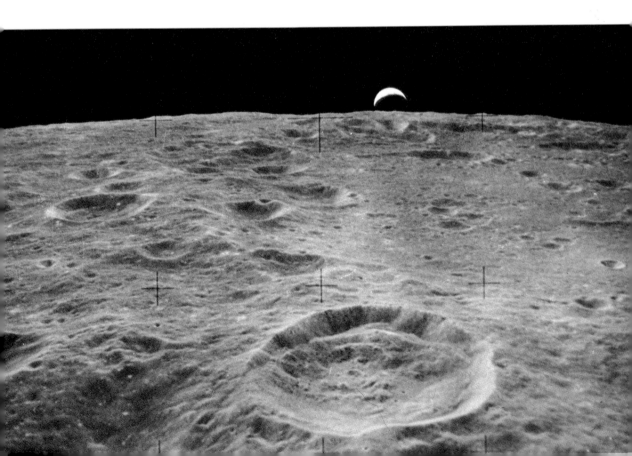

Venus

Venus is often thought of as Earth's sister planet. It is the closest planet to Earth and about the same size. But it would be impossible for us to live on Venus.

The surface of Venus is hot enough to melt lead. The pressure of the atmosphere is 90 times that on Earth. Clouds of deadly acid swirl around the planet.

△ The thick, swirling atmosphere of Venus hides its surface from view. It traps the Sun's heat to make the surface extremely hot.

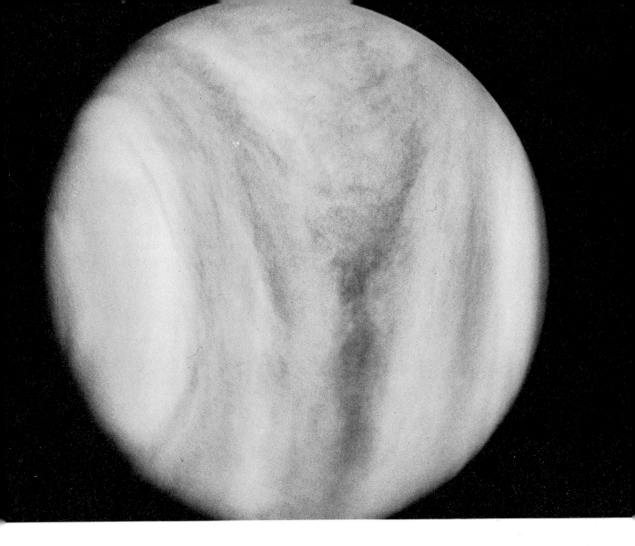

Apart from the Moon, Venus is the brightest object in the night sky. From Earth it looks like a brilliant star.

△ A space-probe photograph of Venus. A special filter on the camera lens produces a better picture through the atmosphere.

Venus spins around very slowly under its heavy atmosphere. A day on Venus is 244 Earth days. It travels around the Sun in about 225 Earth days. So a day on Venus is longer than its year!

Mercury

Mercury is the closest planet to the Sun, and the smallest except for distant Pluto. Its surface seems lifeless and is pitted with craters.

Mercury speeds around the Sun in only 88 Earth days. But it takes 59 Earth days to spin once on its axis. It is difficult to observe Mercury in the sky. Space probes have sent back detailed pictures.

▽ A picture of Mercury built up from photographs taken by the Mariner 10 space probe. It has no atmosphere. In daylight the surface is extremely hot, while the dark side is intensely cold.

Mars

Mars is known as the red planet. Chemicals in its soil give it a reddish-orange tinge. For a long time it was thought that there might be life on Mars. But tests carried out by space probes have shown no evidence of this so far.

There is a very thin atmosphere on Mars. There are small ice caps at the poles of the planet.

△ The Viking 1 space probe landed a robot explorer on Mars. This Viking Lander was able to scoop up samples of Martian soil and test it. No signs of life were found.

△ Dunes on the surface of Mars photographed by Viking 1. Viking discovered many other interesting features on Mars, including canyons, volcanoes and long, winding valleys.

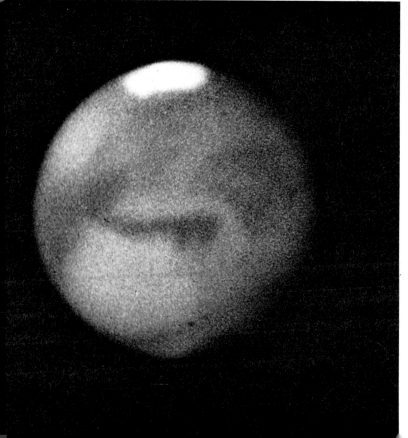

◁ The ice caps of Mars may be clearly seen through a telescope.

Mars is about half the size of Earth. Its days are only slightly longer than Earth days, but it takes nearly twice as long to go round the Sun.

Two small moons, Phobos and Deimos, travel around Mars like huge lumps of rock in space. Phobos is closer to its planet than any other moon in the Solar System, about 5,800 miles (9,300 km).

△ Phobos is a tiny, oddly shaped moon, but looks like a very large piece of rock. It measures about 15 miles (24 km) from end to end.

17

Jupiter

Jupiter is a truly giant planet. It is 11 times the diameter of Earth. A hollow ball the size of Jupiter would hold nearly 1,400 Earths!

Although it is made up mainly of liquids and gases, Jupiter is more than twice as heavy as the rest of the planets put together. It spins around in less than 10 hours, but takes nearly 12 Earth years to circle the Sun.

▷ Jupiter (top right) with its four large moons. Jupiter has a ring, discovered by a space probe. But it can be seen only with the Sun behind Jupiter.

▽ A closer view of Jupiter's swirling clouds and the Great Red Spot (top right). This oval patch, as big as three Earths, is thought to be a raging storm.

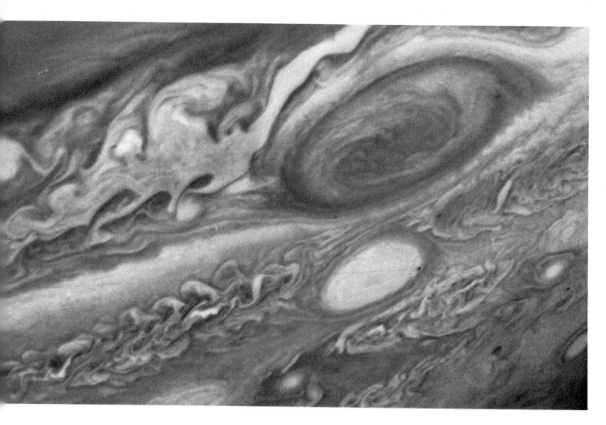

Jupiter is the first of the outer planets. It is five times as far from the Sun as Earth. It took the Voyager space probes a year and a half to reach the world of Jupiter.

The planet has at least 16 moons. Four large and 12 smaller ones have been discovered. Ganymede is the largest moon in the Solar System. It is bigger than the planet Mercury.

△ The moon Io has several giant volcanoes which erupt all the time.

▷ Europa (top) and Ganymede (bottom) both have cracked surfaces. Europa has a smooth surface of ice, which looks like a cracked eggshell. Ganymede is covered with thick ice that has been crushed and pitted into a jumble of icy shapes.

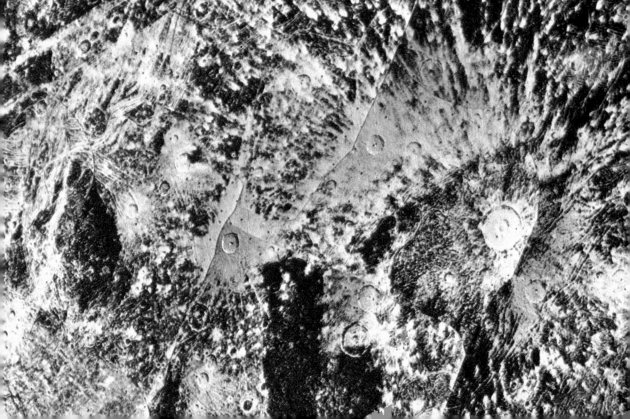

Saturn

Saturn is the most beautiful jewel of the Solar System, as it spins around with its rings like a top in the sky. Like Jupiter, it is made up mainly of gases and rotates so fast that it bulges in the middle.

It is nearly twice as far from the Sun as Jupiter and takes nearly 30 Earth years to circle the Sun.

▷ Titan's thick atmosphere hides its surface in a smoggy haze.

▽ A picture of Saturn taken by the Voyager 2 space probe. The two main rings can be clearly seen, separated by a dark division.

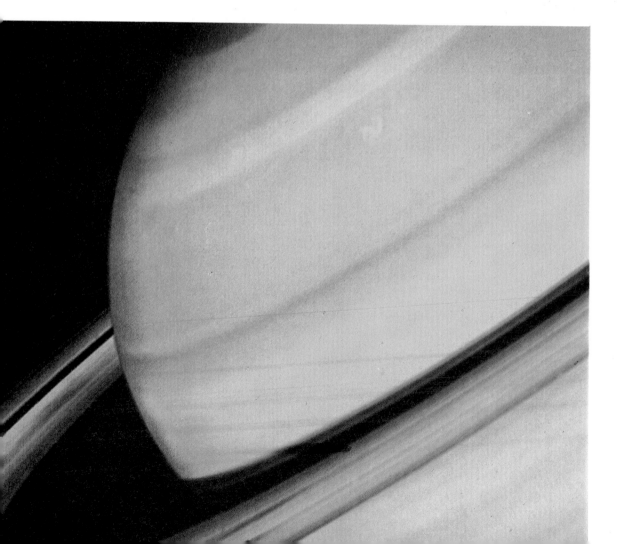

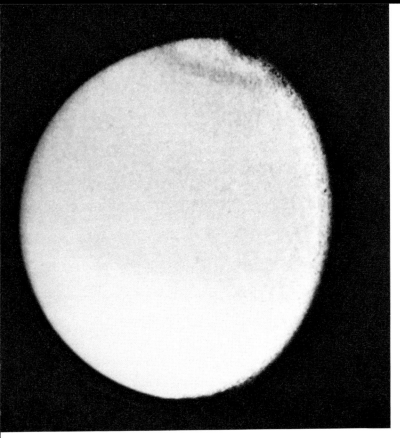

△ Mimas, one of Saturn's many moons, is about one-ninth the size of our Moon. The large crater shown in this close-up photograph is about 80 miles (130 km) wide.

Until a few years ago it was thought that Saturn had 10 moons. But using information sent back by space probes, we now know that it probably has double that.

The most interesting of Saturn's moons is Titan, second only in size to Ganymede in the Solar System and just bigger than Mercury. It is the only known moon with a dense atmosphere. This is thought to be made up of nitrogen and other gases.

◁ A space-probe picture of Saturn's rings. The various colors in this special photograph show up different chemicals in the materials that make up the rings.

The rings consist of millions and millions of small bodies. These vary from particles the size of dust to boulders about 30 ft (10 m) across. Looked at edge-on, the rings can barely be seen, because they are only a few hundred yards thick. But measured across, they would span three-quarters of the distance from the Earth to the Moon.

Because we normally see Saturn from an angle, the rings seem oval-shaped. But they are perfectly circular.

Uranus, Neptune and Pluto

Farther out in the Solar System there are two more large planets, Uranus and Neptune, each with diameters nearly four times that of Earth. But they are so distant that little of their surfaces can be seen clearly even through powerful telescopes.

In small telescopes, Uranus looks like a faint greenish star. It has five known moons and a ring system that was discovered only in 1977.

△ Neptune (bottom right) has two known moons, arrowed in the picture. Triton, which can just be seen underneath the planet, is one of the largest satellites in the Solar System. The distant Nereid can be seen in the top left-hand corner. The starlike appearance of Neptune is due to the photograph.

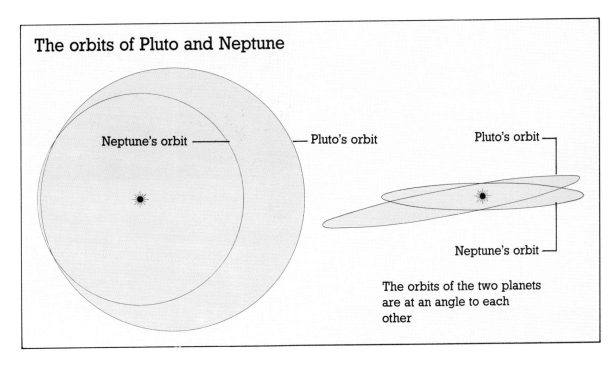

The orbits of Pluto and Neptune

Neptune's orbit ——— ——— Pluto's orbit

Pluto's orbit ⌐

Neptune's orbit ⌐

The orbits of the two planets are at an angle to each other

Pluto is the smallest planet and the farthest from the Sun. It takes nearly 250 Earth years to make one orbit. A moon, Charon, was discovered in 1978.

A collection of about half a million huge chunks of rocky material orbits the Sun between Mars and Jupiter. They are called asteroids or minor planets. They range in size from a few miles to 620 miles (1,000 km) across and have irregular shapes.

△ Pluto has an unusual orbit. The orbits of the other planets are almost circular, with the Sun in the middle. Pluto's orbit is slightly oval, with the Sun much nearer to one side. As a result, Pluto is not always the farthest planet from the Sun. Part of its orbit comes within Neptune's orbit.

There is no danger of a collision, however, because Pluto's orbit is at an angle to Neptune's.

The story of the planets

Ancient astronomers

In ancient times, astronomers thought that the Earth was the center of the universe and that the Sun and planets revolved around the Earth. The only planets known were Mercury, Venus, Mars, Jupiter and Saturn. In the early 1500s, the Polish astronomer Nicolaus Copernicus showed that the Sun was the center of the Solar System and that the Earth moved around it.

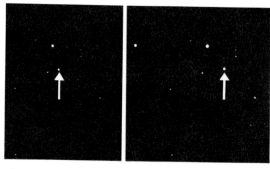

△ These two photographs were taken 24 hours apart. Pluto (arrowed) has changed its position. Only planets, not stars, do this in the night sky.

△ Neptune (right) was discovered because Uranus (left) strayed from the path it should have taken.

Discovering far-flung planets

William Herschel discovered Uranus in 1781, before he became a famous astronomer. Some years later, Uranus began to puzzle astronomers. It was not following its predicted path. Astronomers began to search for an unknown planet that might be pulling Uranus out of its true orbit. They found one in 1846, and called it Neptune.

Pluto was also predicted in a similar way, and found in 1930.

Taking a closer look

There is a limit to what telescopes can tell us about the planets. In the mid-1960s, both the US and the USSR began sending space probes to find out

△ The view of Mars as the Viking 1 probe approached it.

△ The surface of Mercury as seen by the Mariner 10 probe.

more about the planets closest to Earth.

Some probes fly past the planets. Others orbit and even land on the planets. They all send back pictures and other

△ The Soviet Venera 7 probe. In 1970 it became the first spacecraft to send back information from the surface of Venus.

information to Earth. In this way, we have learned much more about the conditions on other planets.

Visiting the giants
In March 1972 the US probe Pioneer 10 began its long journey to outer space. In December 1973 it flew past Jupiter on its way to becoming the first spacecraft to escape the Solar System.

△ A magnificent view of Saturn taken by the Voyager 2 probe.

Meanwhile Pioneer 11 and Voyagers 1 and 2 were launched. They sent back wonderful pictures of Jupiter and Saturn and their moons.

Voyager 2, launched in August 1977, flew past Jupiter in July 1979 and Saturn two years later, on its way to a rendezvous with Uranus in 1986.

Facts and records

△ Olympus Mons, the largest mountain ever discovered.

Mighty mountain

The gigantic volcano Olympus Mons, on Mars, is the biggest mountain so far known to us. It stands 16 miles (26 km) high, 3 times as high as Mount Everest. Measured across, it covers 335 miles (540 km) of the surface of Mars.

△ A Voyager 2 picture of Titan, one of Saturn's moons, showing the atmosphere clearly.

Most moons

The giant planets Jupiter and Saturn have many more moons than any of the other planets. It used to be thought that Jupiter had the most of all. But space probes have discovered that more moons orbit Saturn, possibly as many as 20. Some moons may not have been discovered yet as they are so small or far from their planet.

△ Ganymede, the largest moon so far discovered in the Solar System.

Biggest moons

Saturn's largest moon, Titan, is the only moon known to have a dense atmosphere. It is a little smaller than Ganymede, Jupiter's largest moon, and both are bigger than Mercury.

Ganymede is thought to be the biggest moon in the Solar System, measuring 3,275 miles (5,270 km) across.

Glossary

Asteroids
Small rocky bodies that go round the Sun between the orbits of Mars and Jupiter.

Atmosphere
A planet's outer layer of gas. The air we breathe is part of the Earth's atmosphere.

Axis
A spinning body turns on its axis. This is an imaginary line running right through the center of the body.

Crater
A circular hole or dent in the surface of a planet or moon. Craters are caused either by something that crashed into the surface, or by volcanoes.

Day
The time it takes for the Earth to make one complete turn on its axis.

Minor planets
Another name for the asteroids.

Moon
A body that orbits a planet. Our Moon is the only one the Earth has. Some planets have none, while others have several.

Orbit
The path one body takes around a larger body. The Moon travels in an orbit around the Earth, and the Earth around the Sun. They are said to orbit the other body.

Poles
The two points on a planet's surface that are also on its axis. The Earth has a North Pole and a South Pole.

Satellite
Another word for moon. There are also artificial satellites. These are man-made objects, such as spacecraft, that orbit another body.

Space probe
A spacecraft sent into space to explore and find out more about the Solar System.

Volcano
A round hill or mountain through which molten rock from the inside of a planet or moon flows out. It usually has a central crater and is made of ash and lava that has become solid.

Year
The time it takes a planet to make one orbit of the Sun.

Index